FIND A WAY

F■ND A WAY.

HOW A WATER BOTTLE TOOK ME FROM AMPUTEE TO ALL-STATE

BY BRAD HURTIG

Find A Way: How a Water Bottle Took Me from Amputee to All-State

By Brad Hurtig

Published by Madison Press
Printed by Lightning Source

Edited by Shannah Hogue
Cover Design by Budi Setiawan
Page Design and Layout by Michelle M. White

Hurtig, Brad, 2017
[Find a way: how a water bottle took me from amputee to all-state]
Young Adults / Self-Help / Student Leadership

ISBN 978-0-692-91667-4

Manufactured in the United States of America

Dedication

To my family:
Dad, Mom, Brian, Jeff, and Chris.
And the "sisters" my brothers brought into
the family: Kim, Lauren, and Vanessa.
I'm grateful for all your love and support.

To my close friends who played
an integral part in my story:
Keenan, Nick, and Nathan.
We've been through a lot.

And to a very helpful mentor, Joel Penton,
and my editor, Shannah Hogue.
You guys are incredible.

What's Inside

INTRODUCTION
My Nightmare
1

CHAPTER ONE
Round 1: When I Lost to a Power Press
5

CHAPTER TWO
Round 2: When I Overcame a Water Bottle
19

CHAPTER THREE
How a Guy with No Hands Drove a Golf Cart
33

CHAPTER FOUR
That Time I Got Fake Arms
51

CHAPTER FIVE
How a Guy with No Hands Played Football Again
71

CHAPTER SIX
The Day I Realized I Was Living Again
91

Notes
99

Introduction

My Nightmare

At first . . . I felt nothing. All my senses seemed to shut down.

Slowly, my hearing returned. Sounds began to register. I heard . . . someone screaming. Why? Was it because of me, because of what had just happened?

But what had happened? The press had come down. That was normal. I had heard the brake release and felt the powerful crash that shook the concrete floor. That was right, too.

But no . . . something was not right. I should be farther away. Wait. I had reached into the press to adjust the part. My arms were inside.

My arms were inside.

No. This wasn't real. I couldn't believe it. Surely 500 tons had not just slammed down on my hands and arms.

Panicking, I stumbled away from the machine. My heart pounded against my chest, and my thoughts raced.

Everything was wrong. It was a nightmare. A nightmare I couldn't wake up from. . . .

The Way Through

Adversity is a true equalizer. Nobody escapes the experience of pain. Nobody can avoid being hurt or dealing with difficulties. Eventually, everybody faces setbacks and challenges. And when those moments come crashing into your perfectly laid plans, the nightmare begins.

We wrestle. We resist. We backtrack. We detour. We do everything we can to find a way out. But we can't. I would know.

Adversity came slamming into my life, leaving me floundering in its wake. I struggled to make sense of a life I never asked for. I wanted desperately to go back. I wished for an easier path, but I didn't get it. I had to deal with it, and at some point you, too, will have to deal with adversity.

Thankfully, when the ground starts to crumble under you, as it did for me on that terrible night, there is something you can do. There is a path *through the pain* to an ending better than you ever thought possible. It's a simple strategy, a three-step approach, that helped me move through my nightmare to an amazing life on the other side. I call it Find A Way.

I didn't invent it. Find A Way is a strategy that I uncovered as I lived it. The next step wasn't always obvious. The path unfolded slowly. But eventually, these three steps led me to a life better than I ever thought possible on that horrible night when everything came crashing down.

I invite you to walk that path with me. Let me share with you the three steps that got me through because I am convinced they will be enough to get you through, too. No matter what you face, just like me, you can Find A Way.

Let's get started.

CHAPTER ONE

Round 1:
When I Lost to a
Power Press

 My Kind of Normal

I grew up outside of a small town called Sherwood. Well, it's actually not a town; it's only a village. And when I say small, I mean really small. It doesn't even have a traffic light. A few years ago, there was a flashing caution light at the main intersection, but it got torn down in an accident, and no one ever bothered to put it back up.

I never thought of Sherwood as anything special. It was just my kind of normal. It's in the northwest corner of Ohio, so it shouldn't be confused with Robin Hood's Sherwood Forest. Although, it wouldn't surprise me to see men in green tights come through town someday. The neighboring town is called Hicksville.

Despite its small size, Sherwood wasn't a bad place to grow up. I lived there with my mom and dad and three older brothers. Brian and Jeff are a couple of years older, while Chris managed to join the family a whole two minutes ahead of me.

Being one of four boys was great, and it was a lot of fun growing up with a twin. Over the years, we had a thousand adventures. We spent hours fishing at my grandma's pond, hunted snakes on my parents' property, and created and raced on a mud go-kart track. And we did all the other slightly crazy things that four brothers might do.

When we weren't playing hard, we were working hard. Like our own "Mr. Fix-it," my dad is a do-it-yourself type, so we were always involved in whatever projects he had going on. The biggest one was when I was in eighth grade: My dad practically built our house. Even better, he let us help! We worked right alongside him, and because of him, I learned that I loved to work with my hands. I loved that I could actually build things (like a house), and I even thought that construction might be a good direction for my future.

But back then, my future felt a long way off. I was just a high school student. I went to school, did homework and chores, and—most importantly—I played sports.

My small town had an equally small school, and in order to field full teams, nearly everyone played sports. So, like most guys, I was a three-sport athlete. I played football, basketball, and baseball. And I loved them. All of them. I played with my friends and my twin brother. Sports kept me busy year-round, and I found I was pretty good at them, too. In my sophomore year, I started as the varsity middle linebacker on defense and broke the school record for tackles in a single season.

For the first two years of high school, that was my kind of normal. Sports. Working with my hands. School. Family. I was busy, and life was great.

An Overnight Adventure

But sometimes life changes in the blink of an eye.

It was early summer, and I had just finished my sophomore year of high school. After going to church that morning, my family and I headed over to my older brother's property to clear brush. It was a perfect day filled with sunshine and blue skies. While we were working, my friend Keenan called.

Keenan's dad owned a factory, and he was offering Chris and me a chance to work an overnight shift that night. We loved the idea of helping Keenan and his dad out while also making a little extra money. But we weren't so in love with the idea of working through the night, staying up for twenty-four hours straight, which we had never done. And, more importantly to us, we were concerned about the baseball game we had the next day. The question was, would we be able to work all night and then sleep enough during the day to be rested and play well?

After Chris and I talked it through, we decided, "Yeah, we can handle it." So that's what we did. Later that night we finished up at my brother's and went home. We changed our clothes, and, instead of going to bed like normal, we put on our work boots and got ready to go to the factory.

I was running behind, and Chris was already in the car waiting for me. As I was pulling my bedroom door closed, I heard my mom in the kitchen. But I was in a hurry, and since I would see her again in just a few hours, I didn't stop. Instead of looking at her to say goodbye, I just yelled out "See ya later!" and headed down the hall. I joined Chris in the car, and off we went.

Keenan hadn't said what we would be doing that night, but we weren't too worried. Because of my dad, Chris and I were well acquainted with power tools. Or so we thought. After being introduced to the machine we'd be operating, I suddenly realized I knew nothing about real power.

They called it a 500-ton power press.

A power press is a machine that bends and forms sheet metal into parts, car parts in our case. Until that night, I didn't know much about them, but I quickly recognized two very significant facts. First, these presses are big. Many factories cut out the cement floor and bury them five to six feet into the ground. And even buried that deeply, the press can rise almost as tall as the ceiling of your school's gymnasium. Second, these machines are powerful. It takes a lot of force to shape metal, and the particular machine we were assigned uses 500 tons of pressure to form the sheet metal. You can sit in your car in the parking lot of the factory and feel the vibration every time the machine slams down. It's that powerful.

And that is the machine that Chris, Keenan and I would be operating all night. Since this was our first time working at the factory, Keenan's dad, Kreg, trained us on how to run the machine properly. He provided us with safety glasses and white cloth gloves to protect our hands from the sharp edges of the sheet metal. He watched us for a while, making sure we were doing everything correctly, and when he was certain we were handling the job well, he jumped on his golf cart (he was recovering from a broken foot at the time) and drove off.

It was a little intimidating at first, but we quickly figured out a good system. Keenan put a piece of sheet metal, about the size of notebook paper, into the first station, I moved it through the middle stations, and Chris manned the final station and loaded the finished parts into a box. After the machine came down and stamped the sheet metal, we stepped up to the press, moved the sheet metal in our stations, and stepped back. Keenan would then have to turn his back to the press to reach the buttons. He would press the buttons to activate the machine, and when it was finished cycling, we'd step back up and move the sheet metal again.

Our system worked so well that we started to have some fun while we worked. We talked and laughed and imagined our bank accounts getting bigger. We were going to be paid for the number of parts we made, so of course, we were motivated to make a lot of parts. We enjoyed that every time the press came down and crunched that metal into a part, we were crunching out dollar signs. We even broke into song occasionally: "I'm in the money . . . I'm in the money!" Then after hearing the press come down, we'd give a loud "Heeeeeyyyy!" and throw our hands up, celebrating the money we'd just made.

But even though we were having a good time, the power of the machine constantly reminded us of the seriousness of our job. At one point that night, we actually talked about what would happen if someone got their hands caught inside the press, how it would simply obliterate whatever was inside. Of course, the question was just hypothetical for us. These presses are equipped with safety features, lasers that detect if something is in the way of the press. If those lasers are triggered, the press won't come down. And several times during our shift, that actually happened.

The first time, we were really confused. We stepped back from the press, while Keenan pushed the buttons, ready for the brake to release and the press to come crashing down. Except—nothing happened. It was like pulling the trigger on a gun and expecting that powerful explosion only to realize the safety was still on. We thought something must have broken, but thankfully, that wasn't the problem at all.

Kreg had taught us to spray down the parts in the press every so often to keep the machine lubricated and working smoothly. That time, the spray bottle had been inadvertently placed in the way of the lasers, so when Keenan pushed the buttons, the press didn't come down. It happened several more times, but at least it assured us the safety features were working.

After a few hours, we were really getting the hang of the press. We were getting richer, and we were having a good time. It was turning out to be a fantastic overnight adventure.

Until about 2 a.m.

It All Comes Crashing Down

Have you ever had a crisis moment? One huge moment when something slams into your life and you can't really wrap your head around it yet, but you know—you just *know*—that everything has changed.

We had just come back from a short break. We pulled on our white cloth gloves, put on our safety glasses, and got back to work. Just a couple of cycles in, though, I saw that one of the pieces of sheet metal was crooked. And I knew if the machine pressed the piece when it wasn't straight, it would ruin the part. So I instinctively reached back into the press to adjust it. I didn't say anything to Keenan, nor did I realize that he had already turned around to activate the press.

Even though this was obviously a mistake, the lasers that detected the spray bottle several times earlier in the evening were still in place, and they are there to detect any object that might be too close to the machine . . . like someone standing with their arms inside the press. However, at that moment, I somehow reached in beyond the lasers, clearing them while not being detected. The machine never recognized that I was there.

And while I was adjusting the sheet metal, the 500-ton power press, the machine you can feel come down while in the parking lot, came down—*with my arms still inside.*

The first thing I remember wasn't the physical pain or even a physical sensation at all. What I first remember was hearing someone else screaming. I have no idea whether it was Chris or Keenan or both. All I could think was, *Oh no. What just happened?!*

I started to panic, and I knew I needed help. I left the press to go find Kreg. On the way, I had to look down. I needed to see how bad this really was.

And it was bad.

My left hand was barely there. The press had cut off half of my left hand, including the last three fingers. My index finger was severed almost completely in two. The last half of it was dangling down from my hand, and it looked as if the threads of the white glove were the only thing keeping it attached. It was hard to comprehend that *that* was my hand. But then I looked at my right arm, hoping it was better. It wasn't. It was worse. Half of my arm was missing; it simply ended a few inches beyond my elbow.

What I was looking at seemed like a bad dream.

The entire time, I was fully aware and conscious, but everything slowed down. Any sound I heard had an echo, like it was reverberating around me. It felt completely surreal.

Kreg heard the screaming and started our way. When he saw me, and realized I was missing my hands, he rushed towards me, his eyes wide with shock. I'm sure the sight of me must have blown him away, but all I remember was how calm he was. He very quickly and firmly said, "We need to get you to the hospital." And as fast as he could manage, he led me to his car.

As we hustled out of the factory, I had a brief moment of hope. I knew doctors had been able to reattach severed limbs pretty successfully. But at the same time, I remembered our conversation earlier that evening. A 500-ton power press had just come down on my arms and hands. There wasn't going to be anything left to reattach.

A 500-ton power press had just come down on my arms and hands. There wasn't going to be anything left to reattach.

We got to Kreg's car, and we sped off to the hospital.

The Aftermath

The whole thing felt like a really bad, weird dream. A nightmare. The car ride to the hospital was short, as we cautiously but hurriedly sped through red lights on the way. It was the middle of the night, so the town was dead, but that only added to the eeriness of what was happening. Only moments before, the power press had come crashing down on my arms. But in that car, there was enough time to think and the full force of what had happened hit me.

Physically, the pain was starting to grow. It was a burning sensation, as if the ends of my arms were getting hotter and hotter as we got closer to the hospital. But even that sensation wasn't as intense as I would have expected. The real pain was internal. I tried to wrap my head around the fact that this was real. It happened. And I couldn't change it.

I knew, instinctively, that my future was going to be very different than what I had imagined. My mind went immediately to sports, and I started hysterically saying out loud, "I'm never going to play sports again . . . I'm never going to play sports again!" Being a three-sport athlete, this was a big deal to me. I was the starting middle linebacker, but now I didn't have hands.

During the drive, I started feeling deep regret. I so desperately wanted to go back in time, just a few minutes back, and undo what had happened. I wanted to go back to three buddies working the night shift, talking about guy stuff and looking forward to our baseball game the next day. But I couldn't go back. No matter how badly I wanted to. I was overwhelmed by an extreme sense of desperation and helplessness.

We finally got to the local hospital. Kreg parked right next to the building. He jumped out and hobbled around the vehicle to open my door for me. Then he went into the hospital ahead of me and began explaining the situation to the first person he met at the desk. I could tell there was discussion, and he didn't seem to be getting anywhere.

Then I walked in.

The nurse screamed out, pointing to the room around the corner and telling me to go there. She started calling for assistance on the radio as I went and sat down on the bed. Quickly, someone rushed in and had me lay down. More and more people came, and they all seemed frantically busy. A nurse used large scissors to cut my t-shirt from top to bottom. They started poking me with needles in different places and running lines from one place to another. More and more doctors and nurses arrived, and it felt like I was in the middle of a beehive.

Oddly, the pain still wasn't overwhelming. I just remember a lot of chaos going on around me. At one point, I saw Kreg sitting on another bed across the room. He looked like he had seen a ghost. He was pale and rubbing his chin with his left hand. It was obvious the situation was weighing heavily on him. Eventually, though, somebody pulled a curtain between us.

The hospital wanted to save all that they could of my hands, so they called the factory and requested that someone retrieve any salvageable pieces of my hands that might be left in the press. Like the incredible brother that he is, Chris went back to the press to see what he could find. (I don't know about you, but I think we need more brothers like him in the world.) Unfortunately, there wasn't much to find, just a few finger tips sitting outside the press. Chris didn't miss a beat though. He picked up what he could and put them in a clear plastic baggie for the hospital.

At the hospital, the medical team slowly got me stabilized. The urgency lessened, and there were fewer and fewer white coats running around my room. I didn't know it at the time, but they were prepping me to be transported. I was going to be life-flighted to a larger hospital.

Two important things happened as I laid there, waiting to be moved. First, a guy with long, white hair and glasses came and knelt next to my bed. I didn't know him, and he didn't know me, but he very calmly started talking to me. He was asking about my life: the things I liked doing and my family. I don't remember what all he said to me, but I do remember that his words and presence were very comforting and calming. I never found out who he was, but I am thankful he was there for me.

Second, my parents showed up. They had gotten a phone call—in the middle of the night—that one of their sons had just been seriously injured in an accident and were told to come to the hospital right away. They didn't know if it was Chris or me or the extent of the injuries. They just got there as fast as they could. I can only imagine how awful that car ride was for them.

Seeing them deal with the reality of the accident was hard. Just a few hours earlier, I had said goodbye without even taking the time to look back. Now they were coming to the hospital to see me—without my hands. They were brought to where I was, and someone told them everything that had happened. We were all crying together, and I felt I had let them down. They had given me the best, healthiest start to my life that they could, and now I had ruined it. I'm sure they didn't feel that way, but I did. Still, their presence was incredibly comforting to me. I remember asking my dad about sports, and he said, "Let's just get through this right now." It was exactly what I needed to hear.

Finally, the helicopter arrived. As I was being carted to it, I remember being disappointed. This was going to be my first helicopter ride, but it wasn't the exciting experience I had hoped for. I was loaded into a tiny space in the back. No one else got on except the pilot and a nurse who barely fit in the back with me.

The helicopter spun up and took off, while my parents drove to the hospital where I was being taken. Whether I was just tired or the medication got to me, I fell asleep shortly into the trip. When we landed, I woke up to find my parents waiting for me! Even though I was the one actually flying, they had arrived first. (Maybe I should have ridden with them?!) I was awake enough to talk to them as they unloaded me from the helicopter, but I don't remember any of it. What I do remember was waking up in an unfamiliar hospital room a few hours later.

MAKING IT PERSONAL

1. Have you (or someone you know) experienced a major life crisis? Describe the event and how it affected you and your family.

_____

_____

_____

2. Sports were a very big part of my life in high school.What activities or abilities are the most important in your life? How do you think you would respond if they were suddenly taken away?

_____

_____

_____

3. When you face something hard, what is your typical first reaction? Do you react differently to small things than big things?

_____

_____

_____

4. How have your parents, family, or friends shown up for you in a tough time?

_____

_____

_____

CHAPTER TWO

Round 2: When I Overcame a Water Bottle

 ### Eleven Days

Just days before my accident, my mom took a picture of my dad, my brothers, and me. We were working outside, the five of us, building a huge sliding door for our new horse barn. It was early summer. In the picture, we look all manly, working together without shirts. We look normal. We had no way of knowing that, in just a few days, what we considered normal would change forever.

When I woke up the morning after the accident, I faced a new life. The night before, I'd mostly felt regret, an intense wishing that I could go back in time and undo the acci-

> When I woke up the morning after the accident, I faced a new life.

dent. Starting that morning, and over the next days and weeks, I had to begin to deal with the fact that I couldn't go back. I could not change what had happened.

I spent eleven days in the hospital, which was uncomfortable for me, but even more so for my family, specifically my mom. She stayed with me the whole time, sleeping in a chair by my bed. Because, you know, she's my mom.

While I was there, I got tons of cards. Friends from school and church sent me notes. Even some of the other football teams in our conference sent me messages. I had lots of visitors, too. Friends came to see me, my ex-girlfriend visited (That was fun!), and people who knew my parents stopped by. They were encouraging and supportive. In fact, it became a thing for my visitors to sign the dry erase board in my room, and before long, it was entirely covered. The hospital said we couldn't take it home, but a maintenance guy found out about it, visited me, and said, "I'll be sure to take that down for you." I still have it.

But despite all the attention, those days in the hospital were not about my social standing. They were mostly spent doing the hard work of recovering. I had several surgeries as the doctors tried to save my left hand. They inserted metal pins in an attempt to maintain its structure. They also put a pin through my index finger, hoping it would reattach.

Before long, though, I knew that my left hand was not getting better. Every day the tension in my thumb grew tighter, and I slowly lost the ability to bend it. It also lost all color and became charcoal black. Instinctively, I knew my hand was dying, and it was. Finally, my finger fell off the pin they had put through it. It didn't hurt;

in fact, I remember sort of swinging my arm around, watching it dangle and thinking how odd it was to see my finger like that. It was completely surreal. Unfortunately, my mom was watching me right then, and she didn't think it was too funny. She got emotional, hugged me, and told me it was going to be okay.

I felt bad making her cry, but the idea of losing what remained of my left hand never really bothered me. Maybe that is surprising. But seeing my hand in that condition, I already felt as if it wasn't my hand anymore. To me, it was already gone.

My hand was only one part of my recovery, however.

Losing my arms like that was a huge shock to my body. On top of that, I laid in bed for three straight days, which felt like a hundred days to my body. I had never been so inactive in my life. So when the doctors made me get out of bed to walk, I struggled. Even with a person on each side of me, it took all my energy and focus to pick up one foot and put it in front of the other. It was an odd feeling. I don't know why it was so hard to do, but I made a mental note of that moment. I knew that I would get my strength back, but I never wanted to forget just how low I had been.

I also struggled to wrap my head around what my life was going to be like. Early on, the doctors asked if I wanted to speak to a counselor, but I decided not to. It wasn't that I thought I was fine; I knew I was going to need lots of help and support in my recovery. I just didn't feel like I had anything to talk about at that point.

It was in the hospital that I was first introduced to the idea of prosthetics. The doctors were hopeful about the advancements that were being made and thought that prosthetics would be beneficial to me. But my best information came from Chris. He did a bunch of research about them, and it all sounded interesting. At the time, though, everyone around me was more excited about prosthetics than I was. They were looking ahead and were encouraged by what they found; I was still trying to heal.

It was in the hospital that I was first introduced to the idea of prosthetics.

The hospital became a safe haven for me. I believe I could have gone home earlier than I did, but I didn't really want to. In the outside world, everything was going to be different and challenging. I was worried that when I came home, I would want to go out and do all the things I had done before—like help my dad and brothers work on the new horse barn or zip around on the dirtbike—except now, I couldn't. I didn't want to face that reality. Of course, my family was excited about me coming home. Most of them had taken vacation time from work to be with me. But let's be honest, sitting around a hospital isn't much of a vacation. I understood their excitement to leave, so instead of saying anything, I kept my concerns to myself while I dreaded going home.

Eventually, they released me.

At first, I had to go to hydrotherapy sessions several times a week to try to stimulate growth in my left hand. I'd sit with my hand in this whirlpool of warm water saturated with vitamins and minerals. Other than getting me out of the house, it didn't really do any good. So, finally, the decision was made that my left hand was unsalvageable. I went back to the hospital in early July for surgery to amputate what remained of my hand, shortening my arm so that it ended just above where my wrist should be.

Then I had nothing to do but face my new life, which was not easy.

My (New) Kind of Normal

Physically, the medication I had to take made me very sick. Throwing up was a rare thing for me in my old normal, but after I got home, I threw up two or three times every day for several months. (My record was seven times in one day!) It was rough, and I ended up losing 25 of the 150 pounds I weighed to start with. It got so bad that I had to drink this protein shake they give to old people called Boost, which is like thick, slightly chalky chocolate milk. Thankfully, that did help.

Muscle atrophy was another new reality. I'm sure I'd heard of it before, but I didn't really know what it was. Basically, it's when you don't use your body, or a part of it, so you start to lose muscle mass. The muscles simply deteriorate. Because I wasn't using my arms, I lost a lot of upper body muscle. I had always been in pretty good shape, and prided myself on that fact, so it was hard to see my body just fade away.

I also felt very self-conscious about my new appearance. I'm pretty introverted, and I don't like a lot of attention. So, later in July, when I went to the grocery store with my mom (again, mostly to get out of the house), I could sense people staring at my disfigured body, trying to figure out what had happened. It was really uncomfortable, and I wished I could have hidden inside a bubble or something. Only one person was brave enough to ask, an older guy who simply said, "Corn-picker?" I politely said "No, 500-ton power press." I didn't know how else to respond.

The physical reality of my new life was a constant challenge, so emotionally, I pretty much stayed in survival mode. I was numb, going through the motions, doing what I had to do to get by. Except for seeing my parents arrive at the hospital that first night, I hadn't really cried. But of course, eventually the pain caught up with me.

My body was simply overwhelmed. And so was I.

The physical pain hit me after the July surgery. It was scheduled as an outpatient procedure which, roughly translated, meant I was to come in, let them cut off my hand, and then go back home again that same day like it was no big deal. I must have fooled the doctors into thinking I was tough or something because my body did not recover well from the surgery. The pain was intense, and I ended up staying overnight. Even after I was released, the pain was continuous, and when I was finally home, watching TV with my family, my arm started throbbing to the point I had to leave the room in tears. My body was simply overwhelmed. And so was I.

The biggest emotional pain, however, came a few days later. I was lying on the living room couch; my mom was in the kitchen, and no one else was home. For the first time since the accident, I let myself think about the future. Questions flooded my mind. *Will I ever function independently again? What kind of life will I have? Will anyone want to marry me? If I ever have kids, will I be able to teach them how to play sports?*

But my biggest question was simply *"Why?" Why me? Why now? Why at all? Why this huge, life-changing tragedy that I never asked for?*

I really wrestled with it. But as I lay there, fighting the uncertainty and fear, I slowly found peace. Even as I recognized that this new life was going to be much different than what I would have imagined for myself, one thought became crystal clear.

I was going to be okay.

I didn't know how it would all work out. I didn't know when. But I felt God reassuring me that, somehow, it was going to be okay.

First Steps

Gradually, I started to live my new "hands-free" life. And it was hard. When you have hands, a bad day can be bad. But when you don't have hands, a bad day can be horrible. It was as if I was a baby again—except I was 17. It was really tempting to wallow in self-pity, but I quickly discovered that self-pity wasn't helpful.

> I had to swallow my pride and admit I needed help. That was a big step for me.

Instead, I had to swallow my pride and admit I needed help. That was a big step for me. Thankfully, my family helped with all of my basic needs. They encouraged me. And the fact that I could depend on them meant I wasn't alone, and that took away a lot of my fear.

Still, this new life wasn't easy for my family either. They all wanted to fix my situation, but they couldn't give me back my hands. They watched me struggle to do all the little things I used to do without a second thought, like picking up a spoon or tying my shoes, as well as all the things I once loved to do—like play sports.

Chris, in particular, struggled with that part. We had competed together for a long time, even before we started school. Now, he was playing summer baseball without me, and although the team was playing well, our friends shared with me that he was struggling. His focus wasn't on the game; his heart just wasn't in it anymore.

So when our baseball team made it to the sectional finals, I decided to go to the game. I knew Chris needed me there, and I wanted to go to encourage him. It was a major step for me, and I was excited to go, but I was nervous, too.

As much as I wanted to see the game, going out in public was still a concern for me. I was afraid of the attention I would get, the stares and curiosity of people I would see. When I got there, though, nothing I feared actually happened. These weren't strangers in a grocery store. This was my community. They knew me and my story, and they accepted me—with or without hands.

Because of their acceptance, I really enjoyed the game. Chris and the team played well, and they won! But as happy as I was for them, I was also disappointed. I would have been playing in the game if I still had my hands. Instead, I had to watch from the stands. I did join them on the field for the presentation of the trophy and the team picture, but I was the only one not in uniform. It was strange, and I felt out of place.

After that day, I shifted into a new stage of my recovery. I couldn't just stay home. I couldn't hide. I knew I was ready for something more. I needed an escape route. Something that would help me start moving forward. And finally, I found it . . . in football.

A Showdown with a Water Bottle

I played football from the youngest possible age. From the glory days of two-hand touch at recess, to flag football, to organized football in middle school and high school, the game of football was a big part of my life.

So it makes sense that football was what pushed me into my new life. The process wasn't overly dramatic, like some blockbuster movie version of my life would make it seem. And it wasn't because I ended up making a big comeback, though I did and that was really cool (more on that later). Football provided my first steps into my new life— because I was thirsty.

Football provided my first steps into my new life— because I was thirsty.

The whole thing started when I was still in the hospital. Coach Olwin, our head football coach, came to see me, which I really appreciated. What surprised me, though, was that he talked about me playing football again. *Wait, what?!?*

I am pretty sure that a hospital is the last place most coaches go to recruit players, especially players with no hands. Neither one of us knew exactly what playing again might look like, but he told me I was still welcome on the team. In fact, seeing that I still had two healthy legs, becoming a kicker seemed like one possible option.

It wasn't until late in July that I took him up on his invitation. The team was playing in a seven-on-seven passing tournament. Chris had to be there early, so I had my mom take me out later in the day. I enjoyed hanging out with the team and watching them play.

Everyone was glad to see me, and except for the hot, humid weather, it was a fun day.

The tournament went all afternoon, and after being out in the sun for a while, I got thirsty. So I went over to a trainer and asked for a drink. She picked up a water bottle from her carry tote and aimed for my mouth. With a quick squeeze of the bottle, I got a drink, and we discovered what I thought was a great system. When I got thirsty, I'd ask for a drink, and the trainers would grab a water bottle and squirt some water into my mouth. Perfect!

Near the end of the tournament, though, I was standing next to Coach Shininger, one of the assistant coaches who worked with me a lot, and I was getting thirsty again. There was a water bottle on the ground next to his feet, so I asked him to get me a drink.

Instead of squirting the water into my mouth as the trainers had done all day, he glanced down at the water bottle, then at me, then back at the water bottle. And instead of reaching for it, he looked me in the eye and said something I'll never forget:

"If you're thirsty enough, you'll find a way."

At first, all I could think was, *What?!? I can't pick up the water bottle, Coach! I don't have any hands!* But as he made no move to help me, I realized he was serious. I was going to have to figure out how to do this. I reconsidered my options and thought, *I'll show him!*

I got down on my knees and grabbed the bottle with my two stumps. I stood up and bumped the bottle with my chin to get the right angle, pulled on the cap with my teeth, tilted my head back, and squeezed.

And let me tell you, water never tasted so good.

I bumped the cap closed with my chin and tossed the bottle back on the ground with a grin on my face that said, "Yeah . . . what's up *now,* Coach!"

And for the second time that summer, my life changed. With that one accomplishment, who I was shifted again. I wasn't helpless after all. It was a simple drink of water, yes, but if I could do that, then maybe I could do more.

I hadn't just gotten a drink. I had found a way.

MAKING IT PERSONAL

1. The emotional pain of my injury finally caught up with me in this chapter. Describe a time when the emotional reality of an event or problem hit you full force. How did you deal with that pain?

_____

_____

_____

2. My family was a rock-solid support for me during my recovery. Who can you turn to for support when tough times come your way?

_____

_____

_____

3. Was my coach's response to me ("If you're thirsty enough, you'll find a way") kind or not? Why do you think so?

_____

_____

_____

4. Describe a time when you accomplished something that you didn't think you could do?

_____

_____

_____

CHAPTER THREE

How a Guy with No Hands Drove a Golf Cart

 Find A Way

So, you made it through my story. Congrats! I'm glad you're still with me. Because all of what you've just read—my old life, the accident, the first few weeks of recovery, and the water bottle incident—all of that is background.

From now on, I won't recount what happened every single Thursday in my junior year. I won't tell you about every practice or every doctor's appointment. And you won't have to read any more gruesome stories about surgeries and such. You're welcome.

Now, we get to the fun stuff. At this point, let's shift gears from my story (as awesome as it is) to the amazing discovery I made because of all that I went through. Let's dig in, not just to the details of my life, but to the powerful principles that I began to own as I lived my new life.

After the water bottle moment, I noticed a pattern develop. As each new challenge arose, I worked through the same questions. When I followed the process, I reached my goals and gained confidence to push on to the next goal. When I didn't, I'd end up back at square one. It was the path that moved me through my adversity into my future—into something significant.

It's a process that I call Find A Way.

Getting Where You Want To Go

Find A Way is not a slogan or a catch phrase. It is not some "yellow brick road" or express lane around your problems. It's more than that. It's a map that will help you start (and keep) moving forward so that you can reach your goals.

Find A Way is a clear, practical *strategy* that will help you push through whatever holds you back to achieve something significant with your life.

Of course, you probably hear a lot about how to set and reach goals. And, to be clear, we do need to be setting goals and striving to reach them.[1] In fact, Find A Way won't work if you don't set and achieve goals along the way. But this path I'm suggesting is more than just defining or setting objectives. Find A Way is not just about checking boxes off some master list: Get all A's . . . check. Get a job . . . check. Win the state title . . . check. Those things are all fine and good. But we can't stop there. What we do and what we achieve will never entirely define our best life. That's why Find A Way is so powerful.

Find A Way is a clear, practical *strategy* that will help you push through whatever holds you back to achieve something significant with your life. As fun as it is to check something off our list, we have to focus less on quantity (list all your goals and knock them out one by one) and focus more on quality. Find A Way is the path to a rich, full life. A meaningful life with great value, even if you don't check off every one of those boxes you always thought were so important.[2]

Square One

Find A Way will help you get the most out of life, but the question is, where do you start? Well, there's no real secret to it. You just . . . start. The place where you are, the person you are today, is the only starting point you need.

But maybe you don't think it's possible to dive in. Maybe you figure there's stuff you have to do before you can Find A Way. Other people can just start, but you have to make some money or change your bad habits or be someone important or do some mystical rain dance first.

> The place where you are, the person you are today, is the only starting point you need.

Thankfully, you don't. You don't have to do any of that (especially the rain dance). Really. You just have to step up, step in, and start.

Of course, starting isn't easy. As much as we'd like it to be, it's not. We should expect some difficulty along the way. Remember how, when I was still in the hospital, they wanted me to get out of bed and walk? I could barely put one foot in front of the other. I didn't expect it to be so hard. But finally, I took a step.

You can too. Your start might not be physically hard, like my first steps in the hospital. It might be mentally or emotionally hard. Do it anyway. Even if you don't have it all figured out, you can at least start moving in the general direction you want to go. You can refuse to listen to the voice that says it's all too difficult. You can swallow hard, take a deep breath and then lift one foot, make one choice, try one small change, and—congratulations!—you've done it. You've started.

So we shouldn't expect starting to be easy, but we also can't expect every starting point to be the same. After my accident, my starting point was learning to live without hands. Your square one might be similar: a physical or emotional challenge, a diagnosis, or an injury. But those are not the only places we can start from.

Maybe your starting point is pretty far down in a hole (of failing grades, a rough neighborhood, or a lack of support) that you will have to climb out of. Or, maybe your starting point isn't particularly good or bad. There's no real "adversity"; it's just normal. You're busy with life and school and friends, and it's more comfortable than it is painful. That's a possibility, too.

The thing about your starting point is that it's just that—a place to start. Whether it's fair or equal or easy or whatever isn't the point. No matter what it looks like for you, no matter what your square one is, it is simply the spot from which you begin. No matter how far "down" it seems or how far "up" someone else's spot appears, you can begin, right where you are, to Find A Way.

The Power of Labels

Or maybe you hear someone like me claim "You can Find A Way," like it's all positive and possible, and you think, "No way. Not in my situation. You don't get it. You don't know what I have to deal with every day. Nope, I'm just (*fill in the blank*). I can't Find A Way."

And maybe you're right. Maybe you are the one person who can't Find A Way. Maybe your circumstances or past mistakes or personal temptations are just too much. It's possible . . . but I doubt it. Because your true square one isn't really about your circumstances. In fact, it isn't external at all.

It's your label.

Your label is the word you used to fill in the blank in the first paragraph. And every single person on the planet has one (or more than one). It's the thing that you believe defines you, describes you, defeats you. And it could be one of a hundred different things: ADHD. Nerd. Dumb Jock. Homecoming Queen. Drama Queen. Teacher's Pet. Homebody. Nobody.

Whatever your word, it's a name you were called. It's a description someone used for you. It's the box that other people put you in. And somewhere along the line, you believed it too. *That's just who I am,* you decided. And it stuck.

Labels have to be dealt with. Recognizing your labels, the good ones and the bad ones, is vitally important. You have to know what you're up against.

After the accident, my label was bilateral amputee. That was my starting point. It was a medical diagnosis. It was a literal description. And for a while after my accident, it defined me. I was trapped by it. It was the whisper in my mind on that July day that said, "I can't pick up a water bottle . . . I don't have any hands."

And I know I'm not the only one. Letting our labels trap us is a very common problem, though for you, it might sound something more like this:

> *I'm so awkward . . . no one will be my friend.*
>
> *My girlfriend got accepted to college . . . but with my life the way it is, I'll never go.*
>
> *I can't learn algebra . . . I'm too dumb.*
>
> *No one will ever date me . . . I'm not pretty enough.*

In order to Find A Way, we cannot let our labels limit us any more. Because even though our labels are very real, they do not have to define us.

Even though our labels are very real, they do not have to define us.

Today, right now, my label is *still* bilateral amputee. I lost both of my hands in the accident. They will never come back. I will always be an amputee.[3] But even though my *label* is the same, one very significant thing is now different.

I changed my mind.

That's it. The only difference between who I was that day in July and who I am right now is that I no longer think of myself as limited by my label. It's still my label. But it no longer defines me. I started to think about myself differently.

It All Depends on What You SEE

And that is Step One for everyone who wants to Find A Way. The strategy begins when you *change your mind.* You begin to choose to see yourself and your circumstances differ-

> What we focus on always becomes what we see most clearly.

ently. Because good or bad, what we focus on always becomes what we see most clearly.

If you look for good things around you, it becomes easier to see good things every time. If you look for something positive in each circumstance, you will see more that is positive. When you train yourself to look for the people and moments and events in your life that you can be thankful for, you see more and more of them. You become a more grateful person.

Shortly after I lost my hands, I was lying in my bed thinking about my new life, and I was overcome with . . . gratitude. I know it sounds strange, but I thought about all that I could still do. I still had my legs; I could walk. I could still see and hear. I was alive to enjoy the day and the people around me. I chose to focus on those things, and that choice helped me deal better with my loss.

Of course, this doesn't mean I was glad I lost my hands. And it doesn't mean seeing the positive will cause fewer bad things to happen. Life is unfair, and you will be treated unfairly at times. I'm also not saying you have to be grateful for the bad things that do happen to you. It's just that setbacks don't disable us from being thankful. Choosing to see the good, the positive, the things you *can* be thankful for in the life you have right now becomes a powerful cycle that will keep you encouraged and energized and moving on to ever-greater accomplishments.

But if, on the other hand, you spend your energy thinking you're not talented enough, creative enough, smart enough, good-looking enough, or tough enough, you will only see more proof of your limitations. You'll see nothing to be grateful for. You will keep on feeling inadequate. You'll keep believing that you don't have what it takes. So you won't try (because what if you fail?). You might binge-watch shows on Netflix, but your life will stay stuck right where it is. You'll go nowhere and accomplish nothing.

As hard as it may be to accept, it is not your starting place that determines where you end up. It's not your circumstances or your label. Where you end up is almost entirely determined by what you think about. Especially what you think about yourself.

Choosing to SEE Differently

The Find A Way strategy always starts with a major shift between the way you've been seeing yourself and the truth of who you really are.

Think about my story again. Getting a drink from a water bottle doesn't seem like it would be a life-changing event. But for me, it was. And it wasn't because I'm just a grab-life-by-the-horns kind of guy. It was because that moment was about much more than me getting a mouthful of water.

It was not just a water bottle.

That water bottle was more than a piece of plastic; for me, it was a major **obstacle.** Sure, it was small and lightweight, and I could have stepped right over it. It wasn't literally blocking my way. But actually squirting the water out, getting myself a drink, was a challenge I wasn't sure I could rise to.

But I did. Obstacles may seem big and hard and impossible, but when we change our perspective and focus on the positive, they can become something amazing. They stop being the stuff that stands in our way and, instead, become a doorway to new and better possibilities. They don't hurt us; they actually help us.

For me, that water bottle was a **chance**. It was a chance to make more excuses, to walk away from my coach angry and frustrated that he would embarrass me by asking me to do something I didn't think I could do. At the same time, it was an **opportunity**. An opportunity to shift my attitude. To look a hard thing in the face and see that it was, in fact, possible. Even more important, it was a **choice**. That water bottle represented the choice I would have to make, and then keep on making, to see myself differently and change my actions.

It was so much more than a water bottle. And in rising to meet the challenge that day, I learned an even more significant lesson.

I am more than my label.

Before that day in July, I had concluded that "amputee" was the same as "helpless." I didn't do it consciously. But that's how it happens, and that's what I believed. I unknowingly turned my label (amputee) into a lie about who I was (helpless). And because I had accepted that about myself, I was stuck. Hiding behind my label was easier. It felt safer. But it was also keeping me from the life I was meant to have.

> I unknowingly turned my label (amputee) into a lie about who I was (helpless).

So my coach challenged me. And because of his challenge, I did something I didn't think I could do. And suddenly, everything changed.

Getting my own drink helped me **recognize** the true cost of what I believed about myself. At the time, I was focused on my limitations, on what I'd lost. I was seeing only the negatives. But after the water bottle duel, I realized that my negative outlook would steal even more from me—my dreams, my goals, the rest of my life—if I let it.

The water bottle also helped me to **identify** the excuses I was giving about who I was and what I could do. I wasn't helpless. I was obviously able to get myself a drink, which meant that, up until that moment, I simply hadn't been willing to try. I realized I was choosing the easy route out of fear, that I was not trying things because I might fail, that I really didn't have a good reason not to get my own drink.

Instead, I had to begin to **accept** responsibility for my new life. I had to start replacing the "I can't do that" reel in my head with a new idea: "Maybe I can." I had to try. I had to get down in the dirt and see what could happen. I had to do the work, risk the failure, and start to find out if I could really do more than I thought I could.

And of course, I did. I was much more than my label. I still am. And best of all, so are you.

It's All in Your Mind

Once you change your mind, anything is possible. After the water bottle challenge, I started to wonder if, just maybe, I could do more than I realized. Maybe my mindset was holding me back in other areas as well. So I started trying things. I stepped up and stepped out. Doing that one thing gave me enough confidence to try other things.

Like driving a golf cart.

A few weeks after the water bottle challenge, I was hanging around at a team practice when Coach Olwin told me to get the golf cart we used to move team supplies. (I later found out he was being funny and didn't really expect me to get it. But I thought he was being serious! And I thought it would be cool to drive the golf cart.)

I jogged up to the school where the cart was parked, and my excitement grew. *This was going to be fun!* But when I got to the cart, the key wasn't in it. My first instinct was to go back and tell my coach I couldn't get it. But I really didn't want to do that. I didn't like making excuses anymore. I wanted to figure it out. And that meant finding the key.

I decided to look around. Maybe the key was there, just not in the ignition. And it was! It was in a compartment in the dashboard. But now I had another problem. The compartment had a very small opening, and the key was at the bottom, just out of my reach.

For someone with a hand, it would have been no big deal. They could just reach in and grab it. But for me, it was a real challenge. I couldn't get both of my arms inside and to the bottom. So I stuck my longer arm, my left one, in and twisted my body around to get a good angle . . . and I could reach down enough to *just* touch the key. *Okay*, I thought, *new plan.* Maybe I could slide the key to the wall, pin it against the wall, and slide the key up and out.

So I tried that. I got the key about halfway up and lost my hold on it. It dropped back to the bottom. After a few tries, I got it about three-quarters of the way up...

and lost it again. Every time, the key would drop back to the bottom of the compartment, and I had to start all over again.

I started to wonder what the coaches might be thinking. "Where's he at? Is he stuck? Does he need help?" (Call me competitive but not only did I want to get the golf cart, I wanted to do it quickly.) I thought maybe I should just find somebody to get the key out of the compartment. It could save me some time. The last thing I wanted was for the coaches to come looking for me and rescue me. I started to feel anxious, but also decided to keep trying. And finally, after more tries than I could count, I got the key!

Well, I got it out of the compartment anyway . . . and dropped it onto the ground.

This, of course, presented an entirely different challenge. I got down on my knees, pinched the key between my arms, picked it up, and tried to push it into the ignition. But it wouldn't go in. *Come on!* I thought. *Surely this is the right key.*

I tried to decide what to do. I figured the chances of it being the wrong key were slim. And I still didn't want to ask for help. I'd gotten this close, and I wasn't going to quit now. I decided, *This key has to go in.* I just needed another angle. And a little more force. So I got my foot up and kicked the key in. It went in! (You should have seen my celebration dance.)

It was a major success. And I knew I was only moments away from driving the golf cart back to practice. But there was one more problem to solve. I had to figure out how to start the engine . . . which ended up being harder than I anticipated. The steering wheel and ignition were so close together that I couldn't get both of my arms to the key. After trying different angles, I figured out I could put my left arm through the steering wheel to the top of the key and my right arm underneath the key. Then I was able to pinch just enough of the key that I could turn it. . . .

And it started! I had started the golf cart! (Cue celebration dance #2.)

I pushed it into gear, put my arms through the steering wheel, and took off to where the team was practicing. When I came around the corner of the woods toward the coaches, they all just about fell over. I wasn't sure if that meant they were excited that I'd done it or scared for their lives that the no-handed guy was driving the team golf cart at them.

Either way, I had gotten the golf cart. And that's the whole point.

Rising to the Challenge

I didn't just magically change my mind one day. Left to myself, I might still be stuck in that negative way of thinking. I had to be challenged, pushed a bit, before I could see myself differently. That's why what Coach Shininger did for me was so important.

He wasn't making it difficult just to give me a hard time. Though, for a moment, it *felt* like he was being a jerk—he wasn't. He saw something better and greater in me that I couldn't see at the time. All I could see was that I'd lost my hands, but he saw that I had everything I needed to get the job done. He knew I was more than I was choosing to be, and he refused to leave me there.

So instead of "helping" me, he helped me in a different way. He challenged me. And because he did—with a water bottle, no less—I began to push past those questions. I got a new mindset, a new perspective. I determined that I wasn't a victim of my circumstances, I wasn't broken, and I could do whatever it took to succeed.

And that is exactly what happened. I tried new things. I discovered I could do lots of things every bit as impressive as driving a golf cart without hands. Because I saw myself differently, I was able to achieve things that no one believed I was capable of. Even things I never anticipated being able to do.

> When you change your mind, you change your life.

The same is true for you. To Find A Way, you have to get your head in the game. That's the first step. When you change your mind, you change your life. That was Coach Shininger's challenge to me. And it is my challenge to you.

You have everything you need to take this first step of the Find A Way strategy. Work on your mindset. See who you really are, not just your label. And when your moment of challenge comes, do what I did with the water bottle. Acknowledge the challenge waiting (literally) right in front of you. Accept the risk. Decide that you can do it, you are good enough, you can rise above. And then try.

Every time you do this, your confidence will rise. Your endurance will grow. You will begin to see yourself as an overcomer, instead of a victim, and you will discover courage and tenacity you never knew you had.

Best of all, you will actually begin to Find A Way.

MAKING IT PERSONAL

1. How would you define the term *mindset?* Why is your mindset so important?

2. What does it mean for you to live a meaningful life?

3. Labels can be both helpful and hurtful. What do you think makes the difference between a helpful label and a hurtful one?

4. Do you think that how you choose to SEE the world can actually make a difference? Does positive or negative thinking really affect us?

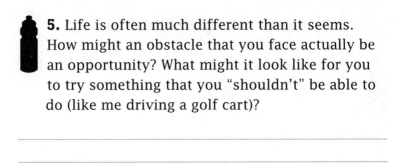

5. Life is often much different than it seems. How might an obstacle that you face actually be an opportunity? What might it look like for you to try something that you "shouldn't" be able to do (like me driving a golf cart)?

CHAPTER FOUR

That Time I Got Fake Arms

 The goal of Find A Way is for you to get where you want to go, and the first step in the process is to change your mindset. But mindset is not enough. If it all just stays in your head, you won't Find A Way. You will still be stuck.

It's like sitting down to play a new video game. You load the game and set your profile. You're all ready to play. But then you don't. Instead of playing, you log out. I guarantee you will never win the game this way.

To Find A Way, you have to move forward. You have to take your new perspective and make it practical. You have to deal with your new reality in concrete ways. In other words, you actually have to *do* something.

Instead of just thinking about stuff, you have to get on the ground and get dirty. You don't just dream and imagine; you set goals and reach them. You don't just create a profile for your new life; you beat the game.

That's why Step Two of Find A Way is to *adapt.*

Adapt Your Life

To adapt means "to adjust (oneself) to particular conditions."[1] It's a change from the way things were to a different way. It means to alter, accommodate, or modify ourselves, our behavior, or our environment so that we can achieve whatever it is we need to get done.

> Adapting is the single most important part of Find A Way.

Adapting is the single most important part of Find A Way. It's the action step of this strategy. It's the part that you have to *do*. There's no way around this step. No one can do it for you. Based on your new mindset, you begin to change yourself and your behavior. You adapt.

Adapting is very practical. There's not a lot of theory here. It's dirty and sweaty and lots of hard work. Adapting is also very personal. Even if your situation is very similar to someone else's, what and how you adapt will probably look very different. Not all solutions work the same for everybody. And adapting is very particular. In order to adapt, you have to be specific, both about the problems that you need to address and the possible solutions you could use to solve them.

Adapting means asking (and then answering) two very basic questions:

1. What do I need to do?
2. How can I do it?

Start by figuring out what you need to get done. Come up with ways to do it. Then try them out. Simple, right?

Okay, I know, it can't really be *that* easy, right? Well, no. Because simple and easy aren't the same thing. The concept is simple, but doing it can be very, very hard.

The actual, real-life process of adapting is not easy in any way. Discovering good solutions can be difficult. And, then, it takes lots of work to actually try out those ideas (one at a time), evaluate them, tweak them, watch them fail spectacularly, and then start all over again. It is very hard. Which is why many people don't do it. They aren't diligent about seeking out all the possibilities. They try a few, obvious solutions, and if those ideas don't work out, they just give up.

To Find A Way, though, you can't give up. No matter how hard it is, adapting is still the only way forward. The key is to keep digging for solutions. Try lots of things. Don't settle for the obvious (but less effective) solution. Be specific and intentional. And never give up.

Mastering the Lunch Table

After my accident, I had a lot to learn. I needed to figure out how to wash myself and comb my hair and pick stuff up again. You know, the basics. But, what I really wanted to do for myself was eat. You wouldn't know it to look at me, but my love of food was legendary long before my accident. Chris and I were known for our ability to pack it away. We used to call dibs on other people's food in the cafeteria in case they didn't eat it, and one time, when we stopped at a buffet restaurant (my favorite kind), Chris and I ate SIXTEEN full plates of food between us. It was awesome.

Obviously, I love food.

So I really needed to figure out how to feed myself again. That was my problem, the answer to Question #1: What do I need to do? And the possible solutions came from everywhere. My good friend Nathan and his dad made me a contraption: a clamp on a bendable post that strapped to my arm. The idea was that I could clamp on a spoon or fork and feed myself. This was a good start, and I did use it a couple of times, but it wasn't ideal.

When I went back to school after the accident, I tried another solution—my twin brother! I would follow Chris through the lunch room while he carried both our trays. We'd find a place to sit with all our friends, and then he would spoon-feed me. Yes, he actually fed me my lunch. Every day. Can you even imagine having someone in the cafeteria of your school literally put your food into your mouth?!?

Well, I can. It was as awkward and embarrassing as you think. But it also worked. I got to eat lunch every day. I asked for the help I needed, and he was (mostly) happy to give it. We adapted to get done what needed to get done. We found a way.

But that solution wasn't a long-term option either. My brother was totally willing to help me, but he wasn't going to be available to feed me my lunch for the rest of my life. So we kept searching.

Eventually, we created the "eater." It was a Velcro version of the contraption that Nathan and his dad made me, but it was much more functional and versatile. It was also a lot smaller and easier to carry around than Chris.

As a side note, Velcro was the perfect material for me. It sticks to itself without having to tie it. It holds together well, but at the same time, I could use my teeth or whatever to pull it apart. And I used it for a lot of things, even going back to Velcro shoes for a while. Although it was a little embarrassing (I felt like some old grandpa), it felt good to be able to put on my own shoes again.

But the "eater" was my favorite Velcro hack. The strap went around the end of my left arm with a slot that I could slide things into. A pencil in the slot let me write. I could flip the pencil around to type with the eraser end. Best of all, I could put in a spoon or fork and eat with it. Chris was out of a job!

And that was how the process went. We kept trying new solutions. We used what worked even while we searched for better ways to get done what I needed done. But all of these solutions were only temporary. From the first days after the accident, prosthetics were always the ultimate goal.

Fake Arms and False Starts

Given my injury, everyone agreed that prosthetics would likely be the best option for me. But even they weren't a perfect solution on the first try. At my very first appointment, the doctors wanted me to consider metal hooks. It was one possibility, yes, but I also know there were many other, more promising options (remember all the research Chris did for me?). As my arms healed, we researched and talked to doctors. It was a long process. I ended up meeting a second doctor, and about five months after my accident, I got prosthetic arms.

About five months after my accident, I got prosthetic arms.

And let me tell you, my arms are so cool. They are surprisingly lifelike; they have five fingers and are the size of a natural hand. Even the outer glove looks a lot like regular skin, with molded veins and wrinkles.

They are also very high tech. They are called myoelectric prosthetics, which is a fancy way of saying that they use the electrical signals in my body to move the hand. They are fitted to my arms, and they have sensors that press against specific muscles. When I tense one muscle, the hand closes. When I contract a different muscle, the hand opens. And they work for me, much better than Velcro or using my twin as my personal butler (as awesome as that was).

Still, adapting myself to my prosthetics was not easy. First, it was a very big change. It was like I was wearing casts on my arms while, at the same time, having to bend wrist muscles to make my hands work. They felt clumsy and unnatural.

Not only that, but I also had to adapt by becoming left-handed. If you've ever tried to use your non-dominant hand for something like eating or writing, you know how awkward that switch can feel. Since my right arm extends just a few inches below my elbow, my prosthetic has to fit so tightly that it limits my range of motion. I can only bend my arm about ninety degrees. But with my left arm extending all the way down to just above my wrist, I discovered I had much more range of motion and control of the prosthetic hand. So I switched and became left-handed!

In addition, adapting is not a quick fix. Because we are used to on-demand downloads, high-speed internet, LTE, one-day shipping, and more, we prefer to have instant results. But that's not how adapting works. It can take weeks, months, and sometimes years to find the right solution. Even when you've found it, you still have to be patient. It will take even more time to make that solution work perfectly for you.

That's what happened with my prosthetics. The goal was to do something every day that I hadn't been able to do the day before. And the process was long and slow and sometimes really hard work. In fact, it was almost two years before I started learning to tie my own shoes again. And even though it's hard to be patient for that long, that is the beauty of adapting. I didn't have to figure it out all at once. I could be patient and keep working, and gradually the adapting happened, one day at a time.

> The process of adapting is hard and takes time, but it works.

The process of adapting is hard and takes time, but it works. Eventually, I put on socks and picked up a spoon. Buffets are once again a favorite hangout. And now, because of my prosthetics, I can live independently. I can take care of my own needs, and I can also do so much more. Like cut my own hair and do a brake job on my car. And run sprint triathlons and play church-league softball. I can live my life. Because I adapted.

You can do the same. Your particular issues will be different from mine. I get that.

For you, adapting might mean changing your diet because of a new allergy or a medical condition. Or adjusting your alarm clock or budget or how you spend your free time. Sometimes, like for me, it means relying on other people to help you for a while. And that's okay. Ask your teacher for assistance or get a tutor or let your brother feed you lunch. It is incredibly brave and hard to ask for help. But it's worth it. Because it's part of the process of adapting. And adapting is the key that lets you Find A Way to do whatever it is that you need to do.

Getting Creative

Adapting begins by defining your problem (Question #1). Then you come up with possible solutions and then try them out until you find just the right one (Question #2). It's a basic, powerful way to get yourself unstuck.[2]

But sometimes, the problems you need to solve are really hard. The solutions will not always be easy to find. You may not have the resources or support you need. So even though you want to adapt, you will still feel stuck.

Those moments can be very frustrating. You'll be tempted to take the easy way out, to give up, to throw down excuses instead of effort. And there were plenty of days I felt like doing just that. But to Find A Way, you can't give up. You have to get creative.

Getting creative means that you have to think big. You think outside the box. You try different ideas, explore solutions that, at first, won't seem possible at all. You consider inventive ways to get things done. And sometimes, to be honest, it will be the crazy ideas that work better than anything else.

> You'll be tempted to take the easy way out, to give up, to throw down excuses instead of effort.

Like elbows.

If you had asked me before the accident how useful my elbows were, I probably would not have known what to say. I mean, they're elbows. But because the ends of my arms were sensitive in the early part of my recovery, I started using my elbows for different tasks. Like maneuvering objects around or picking things up. I'd push myself off the ground with them and use them to activate the mousepad on my laptop. I'm sure that tactic looked odd, but it was a very effective technique. I even took a computer-aided design class while in high school. The class required very fine movements of the mouse to create designs, but I did it! And I did it all with my elbows.

But adapting *myself* was not always enough. I couldn't always change myself to make a solution work. In that case, I had to adapt other things or the world around me to make progress. And that's when creativity became vital.

My phone is a great example.

Prosthetic arms cannot activate a touchscreen, and in case you haven't noticed, touchscreens are everywhere. It was a major problem for me, and there seemed to be no solution. So Chris and I got creative. We swiped dozens of materials across Chris's phone, trying to get something to activate his screen. Some worked better than others, but we finally developed something that worked really well! We put the material underneath the outer glove of my prosthetic hand so it isn't visible, and now I'm part of the twenty-first century! It's great!

Creative solutions are all about finding something that works for you. And that is the primary goal: Find A Way. Your way. Don't worry about what someone else did or can do or would have done in your place. Your problems, your starting place, your circumstances are unique to you, so your solutions can be just as unique. Don't limit yourself to what seems "normal." Try different ideas. Brainstorm with other creative people. Get a little crazy. And don't be surprised when you stumble across exactly what you need to meet the goal you have set for yourself.

Pursuing your Passions

In the months following my accident, I learned how to feed myself and get dressed and take care of myself. But feeding myself and showering is not the sum total of who I am. I am a whole person, even without arms. Before the accident, I loved to be outdoors, playing sports and working with my family. And after the accident, I still loved all of those things.

My passions hadn't changed, only my ability to pursue them. So one-by-one, we began to Find A Way for me to do those things again. And creativity was absolutely necessary to this process.

The best example is my ATV. Before my accident, my brothers and I had dirt bikes that we rode all over our property. After the accident, my brother Jeff wanted to see me back on the trails. So we looked at all the options and figured an ATV would be the best solution. I could sit (instead of balance) on it, and handling would be much easier. He even researched which ATV would be best for me. And it was perfect . . . except for one thing. Most ATVs have a thumb-operated throttle, a button you push to make it go faster, and my prosthetics can only open and close. I can't push a button and hold onto the handlebars at the same time. It seemed I wouldn't be able to ride after all.

So Jeff got creative. He changed out the button throttle for a twist-type throttle, similar to what a motorcycle has. And . . . I could ride again! I won't even try to describe to you the feeling I had when I rode that ATV for the first time after my accident, but I will say that my excitement went beyond a celebration dance.

Riding with my brothers had seemed an impossible feat, and it certainly wasn't necessary. It wasn't basic like feeding myself or getting dressed. But it was important anyway. Having that ATV allowed me to do something I enjoyed, just for fun. It took some creative, out-of-the-box thinking. But it was totally worth it.

Pursuing what you're passionate about is vital. Whatever your passions are, they help make you who you are. They will also help you Find A Way. Your passions provide joy and release and fun that will enable you to move forward even more purposefully, especially when things get tough.

Because things are going to get tough.

Facing Failure

When you are working to achieve your goals, when you are doing the hard work to Find A Way, you will face tests. Finding solutions, adapting yourself and your world, takes a lot of trial and error. You will make mistakes. Many, many mistakes.

It's like Belle's dad from *Beauty and the Beast*. Maurice is this crazy inventor guy who tinkers in his basement, trying to build new and useful inventions. But they're a little, um, iffy. And everybody in town thinks he's crazy because he regularly blows stuff up.

He makes a lot of mistakes. All inventors do. And that's important because you are an inventor, too. You're trying to create the life you want to have, and you do that by setting a goal and then going after it. You adapt. You get creative. And just like Maurice . . . things will sometimes blow up in your face.

Remember my ATV?

One day after my brother had changed the throttle, I was riding around, and I drove into some woods. Which I had done hundreds of times before. However this time, I accidentally drove over a low-hanging tree branch. And things went crazy. The ATV's wheel pulled down on the branch, and the whole limb suddenly came crashing down and hit my arm. The same arm that was twisting the throttle. It smacked my arm so hard that it made me *completely* twist the throttle. And that was a bad thing.

You will make mistakes. Many, many mistakes.

The engine revved as high as it could, and the ATV took off. The sudden burst of speed threw me backwards with enough force that both of my arms pulled out of my prosthetics, *leaving the prosthetics attached to the handle bars!* I held on with my legs as the ATV careened into the woods.

After dodging several trees, I finally managed to lift the prosthetic enough to release the throttle and slammed my foot on the brake. I got the ATV stopped, right before I hit a tree—head on. I sat there, shaking all over, trying to wrap my head around what had just happened. After I caught my breath, I pushed my arms back into my prosthetics and very slowly drove back to the house. I put the ATV away . . . and didn't touch it for a month.

That day I gave all-new meaning to the phrase "Look Mom! No hands!" Of course, I didn't actually tell my mom about that story (moms know a lot, but they don't need to know everything). I know I could have been seriously injured, but the reality is epic fails are sometimes a part of the process. They happen, but they aren't the end. I have made lots of mistakes. Some were little. Some of them were pretty big, but I kept trying and learning from my mistakes. And eventually things went much more smoothly.

My prosthetics are another great example of this learning curve. I had to make a lot of mistakes in order to learn to use them well. Like the time I was getting something out of the oven and scraped my prosthetic hand against the 400-degree burner. Ouch! Well, not really. It didn't bother me since I couldn't feel it (at least one positive to having fake hands!), but the black smoke and the melted plastic told me I needed to pay closer attention next time.

I made the most mistakes learning to use my prosthetics' proportional control. Proportional control means that the strength of my grip matches the intensity of my muscle movement. The harder I push my arm muscles, the harder the hand clamps down. And that ability is great because I can manage how much force I use to pick something up or shake hands or hold something.

But it wasn't easy to learn. Even now, I have to see everything I pick up to make sure that I have a good grip on it or that I'm not squeezing it too tightly.

Like a hot dog.

To be fair, it was the first hot dog I ate after I got my prosthetics. I was at a bonfire and walked over to get some food, including a hot dog. I could tell people were watching me, wondering how this attempt was going to go. And it went great. I got my food, even managed to put ketchup on the hot dog, and went to sit by the fire. Once again, I could tell people were curious and still watching me, but I was hungry. I reached down, squeezed ever so gently on the hot dog, picked it up, and took a bite. No problem! I put the hot dog back down on my plate and started talking to some more people. After a while, it was time for a second bite. So I reached down, squeezed the hot dog as softly as I could, picked it up, and took bite number two. Success! But this time, instead of putting the hot dog back down on my plate, I continued to hold onto it. And . . . I lost focus. While I was still talking, I suddenly realized everyone was staring at me again. This time with their mouths open.

Failing does not make you a failure.

I looked down. I had a death grip on the hot dog. I was crushing it, squeezing the hot dog out of its bun and covering my pants in ketchup. It was glorious.

So what did I do? I got another hot dog! I tried again. And here's the thing: That's exactly what each of us has to do. We try something. And if that doesn't work, we try something else. And then something else. Until we get it. We cannot short-circuit the learning process. We will mess up. But when we learn from those errors, we will eventually get it.

The ability to learn from your mistakes is really huge if you want to Find A Way. To achieve the goals you want to reach, you must grasp this principle: Failing does not make you a failure. Let me say that again.

Failing does not make you a failure.

Failing means that you tried something and it didn't work. It's a mistake. A goof. A crushed hot dog with ketchup on your pants. Being a failure, on the other hand, means that you see yourself as incapable of ever succeeding. And that is a much bigger problem.

Just like in chapter three, our mindset makes all the difference. A true failure is someone who gives up—on themselves, their goals, the life they want to have. They see themselves as a person who cannot succeed—so they don't. They've decided they can't hack it. They see all the things they tried that didn't work, and they stop trying altogether.

But to Find A Way, you have to accept the reality that you will fail, and that those mess-ups do not have to stop you. Achievement happens when you keep going, in spite of the most epic fails you can imagine, until you reach the goal you set for yourself.

I rode the ATV again. We tried dozens of materials until we found one that would work with a touchscreen.

I don't squeeze hot dogs into oblivion anymore. I learned to do things I thought I might never get to do. And so can you.

With the right mindset and a commitment to keep trying, we adapt. We move forward. And when we do, we open up countless opportunities for ourselves. We discover amazing chances to really live. And once you begin to move forward that way, I can tell you, absolutely nothing is beyond your reach (pun completely intended).

MAKING IT PERSONAL

1. Have you ever had to adapt to something new or difficult in your life? Describe what that was like.

2. Do you consider yourself a creative thinker? If not, who could you ask to help you come up with creative solutions?

3. Do you tend to compare yourself with other people or are you willing to deal with your challenges in a way that works for you, regardless of what others are doing?

4. Failing is part of the adapting process. Do you agree with my statement that "failing does not make you a failure"? Why or why not?

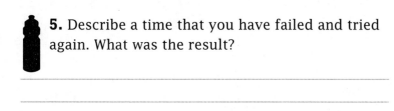

5. Describe a time that you have failed and tried again. What was the result?

_____

_____

_____

CHAPTER FIVE

How a Guy with No Hands Played Football Again

 You can Find A Way. It is possible. But it is not a one-time event. We'd all like to find some magic wand we could wave around and fix our problems all at once. But that's not how life works. And that's not how Find A Way works either.

There will be moments when you conquer a particular challenge or achieve some significant result. In a single day, my prosthetics changed my life, almost entirely for the better. But I'm still learning. I still grip things too tightly or drop things I'm carrying. I'm still finding better ways to use my prosthetics and make improvements to accomplish what I want to get done (like my touchscreen thumbs).

Find A Way is not a single event. It's not just about "the one time you did that one thing." It's a process. It's constantly repeating. As we realize that how we see ourselves or our world has held us back, we change our mindset. Then we adapt and try things; we get creative and deal with our mistakes, big and small. And then we do it again.

We have to be willing to repeat the process in order to Find A Way. And this is Step Three in the strategy: We have *to persevere.*

Driving Forward

I am a firm believer in the simple power of moving forward. I mean, I drove a golf cart a couple of months after losing my hands. And let's not forget the ATV stunt in the woods (ask me later about the stunts I decided shouldn't go in the book).

Obviously, moving forward is necessary if you want to get where you're going. You can't sit in your garage or by the side of the road and expect to get to the restaurant where your friends are all planning to meet up. You have to actually get in your car and go.

Unfortunately, though, life isn't always like a quick trip to the buffet restaurant. We want to move forward, but circumstances and people and bad decisions can all work to keep us stuck in one place. Like me trying to drive the golf cart, we have to find the key before we can move ahead and achieve our goals.

> Perseverance means that you press forward and keep going.

The key to Find A Way is perseverance.

Perseverance means that you press forward and keep going. Even when things are hard. Even when nothing is smooth. It isn't easy, but you keep doing it. You get through the day. You run one more lap. You study for fifteen more minutes. Then you get up the next day, and you do it again. In the sun, in the rain, whether anyone goes with you or not—you go forward no matter what.

That small phrase is the heart-beat of perseverance: no mat-ter what. You do all the normal things, all the small things, all the hard things—and you do them *no matter what.*

> Perseverance begins by stating the goal.

You still have to go to class, but now you have to do it with a dyslexia diagnosis. You have to go to school even though everyone knows your parents just announced their divorce. You head to practice even though you can't kick an extra point for the life of you. No matter what is creating potholes in front of you, you strap on your helmet and get moving.

You can change your mindset. Even adapt. But ultimate-ly, whether or not you Find A Way will come down to whether or not you stick with it. Whether you refuse to give up, even when you really, really want to. Whether you keep moving forward, no matter what, until you finally uncover the life you ultimately want to have.

The Map

Perseverance doesn't just happen, however. You can't just wing it and hope you'll have the willpower to see your goals through. Perseverance takes work, and if you want to Find A Way, you will need a plan.

Having a plan is the basis for every success. A few years ago, I decided to run a marathon. But I didn't just sign up for the next available race. I didn't run 26.2 miles on day one. I made a plan. I had a running schedule with days of rest and days of cross training. Every week, I added longer runs while maintaining my base conditioning. I followed the plan and built up my endurance, and on race day, I ran a marathon.

Perseverance works the same way. Just like you have to train your physical muscles to run a race, you have to train yourself to develop perseverance. You have to *learn* to do it. And that means that you need a plan.

It looks like this:

1. Define the Goal
2. Determine Your Process
3. Do It (Over and Over Again)

If you want to see more perseverance in your life, in any area, that's the roadmap you need to follow. If you don't believe me, if you're shaking your head like I'm crazy, that's okay. I can prove it. Following that plan is what helped me develop the perseverance I needed to move from amputee to all-state.

1. Define the Goal

Right after my accident, playing football again wasn't an obvious goal for me. In fact, when Coach Olwin invited me to stick with the team that day in the hospital, I pretty much thought he was crazy. But as absurd as a no-handed man playing football seemed, having a goal was a powerful motivator for me. It gave me a clear objective, something to work toward. And it worked. I did rejoin the football team that fall.

To be fair, I could have been "on the team," suiting up and standing on the sidelines, but not actually playing. But that wasn't going to work for me. I was not interested in being a glorified mascot. If I was on the team, I wanted to play. And the coaches wanted to help me do just that.

So we defined the goal.

It wasn't just to wear the uniform again or stand on the sidelines. I wanted to play middle linebacker again. In fact, I wanted to *start* at middle linebacker again. Yes, it was crazy. It was way beyond what I could do in the fall after my accident. But it was the goal that I intended to drive toward. It was specific. It was straightforward. I knew what I wanted, and I was willing to push forward until I got there.

You can do the same. For every person trying to Find A Way, perseverance begins by stating the goal. What do you want to accomplish? In what time frame? What is your end game?

You can't wander aimlessly and call it perseverance. It doesn't work like that. Perseverance has to be focused to be effective. You have to have a clearly defined goal to pursue. You have to know where you're going; you need a target to shoot for.

Too often, we shrink from saying out loud what we really want to accomplish. It sounds so official if we tell our parents or friends or post it online or write it down in our journal. Defining your goal is scary. And risky. We could fail. Someone might laugh at us. I mean, if we really own up to the thing we want to achieve more than anything else, we make ourselves really, really vulnerable.

Do it anyway. As scary as it feels to define your goal, it's absolutely worth it.

2. Determine Your Process

But the goal itself isn't enough. Perseverance also needs some direction, some clear guidance. You have to determine how you are going to get there, and you need to do it before you actually start.

Determining your process at the start is important for the same reason we check Google Maps when we're driving somewhere unfamiliar. We know the destination, but not the specific details. Knowing the directions keeps us from getting off course. It keeps us from making wrong turns. It helps us move forward in the right direction so that we eventually reach our destination.

Determining your process means taking the goal you want to reach and then breaking it down into manageable pieces. We need small, doable actions to keep moving forward. Many of these actions are baby steps. Some of them will take a whole lot longer to achieve than we want them to. But determining your process ahead of time is vital if you want to actually reach your goal.

The first part of my process was physical. I was surprised how quickly my stamina and strength had disappeared after my accident. To be ready to play, I needed to get back into shape. This involved a lot of running and weight training. And it wasn't easy. My first attempt to jog some laps around the track ended after one lap. I was exhausted. I sat down and told the trainers I was done for the day. In the weight room, I focused on my core and my legs instead of doing bench press and upper body lifts. I used different machines, extra heavy ankle weights, and medicine balls. Slowly but surely, I rebuilt my stamina and strength and even regained the weight I had lost.

This physical part of the process also involved adjusting to my new shape, literally. The first time I ran after my accident, I felt very awkward. It probably didn't look as weird as it felt, but my arms were now different lengths and weights, so I had to relearn how to carry myself effectively as I ran. And on top of all the regular football equipment, I now needed special pads for my arms. Because my prosthetics are made of steel, I couldn't wear them on the field. I guess the referees were worried I'd have an unfair advantage and start clubbing people to death or something.

A second aspect of the process was to create a support team who could advise and assist me with each new stage. I cannot stress enough how important it is to have a strong support system. Perseverance is much, much easier when you have people who encourage you every step of the way.

My family was a big part of this support system. But my football coaches also played a huge role in the entire process. They were the ones who took each goal and broke it down into manageable pieces. They encouraged me. They pushed me every day to do something that I couldn't do the day before. They added the "tough love," the do-it-even-though-you-don't-feel-like-it motivation I needed. And because they were helping me, I stepped back out onto the field . . . as a place kicker.

That move was the last aspect of my process. In order to be ready to play middle linebacker *someday,* I needed to start playing somewhere today. And we settled on place kicking.

The coaches figured that, first of all, kicking would be a safe place for me since I would only kick the extra point after a touchdown. I'd be off the line of scrimmage, away from all the 200-pound linemen. (If you think about it, how often do you see a kicker get hit?) Second, we figured kicking would be a good confidence builder. I could play, have some success, and then carry that confidence over to the next goal. Also, I had played multiple positions and was fairly athletic, so we figured I would be able to kick a football.

But despite all those solid reasons that kicking should have been a great start for me, I struggled. Instead of finding an obvious route to middle linebacker, the process we created almost fell apart. Which brings us to the final stage of developing perseverance: the part where you actually have to persevere.

3. Do It (Over and Over Again)

Only a few weeks after I managed to drive a golf cart without hands, I was pushing myself forward as a kicker. I was learning new skills. I was working hard. And I found out that even with a clear goal and a solid process to guide me, perseverance is not easy.

Being a place kicker is not a hard job, in theory. The ball is snapped, and someone holds it in place so the place kicker can kick it through the uprights for the extra point. Easy, right? Not so much. From my first kick in practice, I knew, along with all my coaches and teammates, that I wouldn't be a kicker. No matter what I tried, I found it really difficult to send the ball a mere seventeen yards for an extra point. I even read articles and studied different kicking techniques. I practiced and practiced and practiced. I put everything I had into it, but I never really got consistently good at it.

But I knew what my end goal was. I knew this was one stage of the bigger process, so I kept at it, and finally, I got an opportunity to kick in a game. It was a big deal, and the whole crowd knew this was my comeback moment. As soon as I started to jog onto the field, everybody stood up

I knew this was one stage of the bigger process, so I kept at it.

and cheered, like we'd just pulled off a sweet victory—except it was just me walking onto the field.

I cannot even tell you how great that moment felt. It was incredibly exciting. We lined up, and I counted off my steps. I took a couple of deep breaths and called for the snap. Everything looked good.

But I missed it. Straight up the middle and seven yards short.

Disappointed doesn't even begin to convey how I felt at that moment. Not only had I not made the kick, but I let down my teammates and the crowd who had celebrated my return. Everyone still cheered for me as I left the field, but it felt like a mercy clap. You know, "Oh, nice try. We feel sorry for you, so we'll clap."

But I also knew I wasn't done. Perseverance means driving forward, not giving up. So I went back to practice and kicked some more. And I got another shot. We ran onto the field. The crowd was on its feet cheering for me again. I lined up, called for the ball, and kicked right through it. And I missed again.

Everybody cheered me off the field, and they cheered again when I got my third shot. But I felt as if I was letting them down. I was desperate to make it, to give them something they could actually cheer about this time. Third time's a charm, right? Nope. I kicked it wide left.

At this point, perseverance seemed like a very bad idea. I was very, very frustrated. I stood on the sidelines and thought, *This can not be happening. Why can't I get this? Can I actually even do this? Will it ever happen?*

And maybe you know how I felt. Maybe you've faced that self-doubt and discouragement. You're trying. You're thinking outside the box. You are doing your best to Find A Way, but you keep falling short. And you're ready to throw in the towel and be done with the whole thing.

That's where I was. And I could have given up right then. Walked off the field with the team and never come back to practice. No one would have blamed me. Maybe a return to football really wasn't a feasible goal. After all, if I couldn't kick an extra point, how in the world was I ever going to play middle linebacker again?

But I didn't quit. I chose to persevere. My coaches encouraged me. My teammates stood with me. The crowd kept cheering for me. And I knew I could not walk away. Not yet. I went back to practice and started kicking again.

Finally, I got another chance. It was my fourth attempt. I jogged out onto the field, and the crowd was . . . trying. They cheered, but I imagined them thinking, "Are we really going to do this again?"

One more time, we lined up. I took a deep breath and called for the snap. It was another good snap, another good hold, and I kicked through the ball . . . and I MADE it!!!

Our crowd went crazy, my teammates went crazy, even the opposing team's crowd was cheering. I was beyond excited. I ran over to Coach Shininger and gave him a big hug, and he said, "You're done kicking! You're moving on to the next goal."

We both laughed. I think he was as excited as I was that I didn't have to be a kicker anymore. I mean, I was one-for-four, so armless or not, I would have told me to move along, too. But that wasn't really the point. I wasn't giving up, and neither were my coaches. They kept pushing me. They never let me settle. And with my career as a kicker happily behind me, we began preparing for my return to middle linebacker.

Persistently, we worked through each action step. We made sure the new arm pads actually worked and protected my arms. I worked to develop enough agility and balance, stamina and strength to play. Of course, I had to prove my ability to tackle, too. We used several different drills to be sure I could still take people down. And I passed.

My actual technique was the same as my teammates who still had arms. I just had to be more disciplined. I couldn't get caught leaning out to tackle someone with only my arms. Instead, I needed to stay low, lead with my shoulder and wrap my arms while driving them to the ground (oh, the joy of a good tackle!).

Once I had demonstrated my ability to tackle successfully, I got the opportunity to play middle linebacker a few times during my junior year. And in the last game of that year, I made an open-field tackle. There was nothing between the wide receiver who had the ball and the end zone. Nothing, that is, except me. If I didn't make the tackle, it would be a touchdown for the other team. I sprinted toward the receiver, got low, hit him with my shoulder, and drove him to the ground. It was awesome. And suddenly, I was sure I could do this.

My confidence rose, and I went into the off-season ready to work hard. I prepared and practiced, and finally, for my senior year, I once again became the starting middle linebacker.

Less than two years after finding myself living a nightmare, it was literally a dream come true.

I had achieved my goal. It wasn't easy. I felt like quitting more than once. It took work and sweat and perseverance, but I did it. And not only did I start and lead the team with 111 tackles that year, I was also named first-team all-state linebacker for Ohio.

Less than two years after finding myself living a nightmare, it was literally a dream come true.

Pursuing Perseverance

You will never Find A Way without perseverance. You have to keep going. No matter what mistakes you make. No matter what roadblocks pop up. No matter who says you can't get it done. No matter how many times you have to try to kick an extra point. Keep going. Find A Way.

But is that really all there is to perseverance? Yes, I told you my football stories. Yes, I gave you the three parts (Define the Goal, Determine Your Process, Do it).

Yes, I make it sound so easy when it's all just some words on a page.

But perseverance isn't easy. It's really, really hard to keep going, no matter what. So the more important question is always "How?" How do we develop perseverance? How do you ensure that you keep going until you reach whatever goal you've set for yourself?

You need three things.

A Firm Foundation

It is absolutely necessary to have a good support system. I've already mentioned this, but it's fundamentally important, so I'm saying it again. You have to have a support team if you are going to persevere.

These are the people who let you mope for a minute and then push you to keep going. These are the people who help you up and encourage you when you're down. They give good advice, clear direction, and the occasional swift kick in the pants. Most of all, these are the people who believe in you, no matter what.

A great example is Bob Bowman and Michael Phelps. The most decorated Olympian ever, Phelps thrived because of Bowman's support and discipline. They trained together for almost twenty years, and Bowman pushed and prodded Phelps, helping him do phenomenal things. Without Bob Bowman, Michael Phelps's story would have gone much differently.[1]

That's what a good support system does. My coaches, my family, my friends, and my teammates helped me achieve the life I wanted. They pushed me. They encouraged me. They worked with me, and when I reached a small goal, they gave me a new challenge. I absolutely could not have done what I have accomplished since my accident without this team of people behind me.

You will need the same thing. Find people who will support you. Don't let anyone tear you down or try to hold you back. Get the help you need. You may not have a built-in support system like I did. In that case, you're going to have to seek those people out instead.

> Perseverance is always easier with a team.

Ask someone to mentor you, tutor you, work with you. Reach out to an older cousin or relative. Ask a teacher or coach or youth pastor to meet with you. There are people around you who want to see you succeed. And if they are not where you are, go to where they are.

You can Find A Way, but perseverance is always easier with a team.

A Good Laugh

The second thing you need in order to develop perseverance is a sense of humor.

Laughter is a powerful and effective coping mechanism.[2] It helps us physically by releasing endorphins and reducing cortisol levels.[3] It helps us emotionally by undercutting our stress and anxiety. And it gives us a more realistic perspective on our situation; we remember that life is more than the challenge that we face at that moment.

During a Q&A session after one of my talks, I had a student ask me, in a concerned voice, how I could make fun of myself. My response was simple: "If you can't make fun of yourself, then you're taking life too seriously. You are not living life to the fullest."

I still believe that. If you cannot laugh at yourself and your mistakes, you will not persevere. The heaviness of your failures and mistakes (real or imagined) will overwhelm you, and you will give up. But when you remember to laugh, you lighten that load.

> If you cannot laugh at yourself and your mistakes, you will not persevere.

Dr. Cynthia Thaik, a holistic health doctor, noted, "We all have obstacles in life and we all make mistakes. There is no reason to beat yourself up over it. Stressing about something you can't immediately change will only make matters worse. In fact, if you can laugh light-heartedly at your own foibles, you'll find that you give yourself that extra happiness and confidence boost that can get you over any hurdle."[4]

Thankfully, humor was (and is) a regular part of my life, and it made a huge difference in my attempts to Find A Way, in life and in football.

During one football game, my friend Randy was on the sidelines with a possible concussion. As they were checking him out, I jumped right in. I had on my football arm pads, which have a rounded foam end, and held one of them up in front of his face. Very seriously, I asked, "All right, how many fingers am I holding up?" Randy looked intently at my pad for a minute, and then he burst out laughing. (Okay, first his eyes crossed a little, and then he laughed.)

Even now, I use humor any time I get the chance. I love it when someone reaches for something hot and then quickly drops it with an "Ouch!" I immediately reach for it, look confused, and say something like, "It doesn't seem hot to me." Those kinds of jokes always bring a laugh.

We need to let ourselves laugh. It makes an amazing difference, especially when you are trying to Find A Way. No matter how dark your day might seem, finding (or creating) light-hearted moments will empower you to persevere.

The Path of Most Resilience

The final ingredient for perseverance is resilience. According to the American Psychological Association, resilience is "the process of adapting well in the face of adversity, trauma, tragedy." While resilience doesn't stop you from feeling sad or hurt by difficulties, it is the ability to "bounce back" when tough times come.[5]

Resilience is a tool shed—like my dad's workshop back home. He has hammers and saws, drills and bits, power tools and hand tools; you name it, it's there. No matter what project he has going, he can go to that shop and pick up exactly the tool he needs. And when a project doesn't go exactly as he intended, which happens sometimes, he heads back to his shop to get a better or different tool so he can finish the job.

> The most important thing about resilience is that *it can be learned.*

That's exactly what resilience is. It is an arsenal of skills, abilities, and attitudes that you can draw from when things get tough. It helps you adapt, get creative, and push forward through each new difficulty because resilience involves a wide range of tools that work in a variety of situations.

One of those skills is the ability to separate yourself from your circumstances. Another is the ability to set and meet goals (even very small ones). Other tools include the ability to be flexible, the ability to manage your time, the ability to communicate what you need and how you feel. These tools, and others like them, are life skills that will help you deal with whatever comes your way.[6]

But the most important thing about resilience is that *it can be learned.* Maybe you don't do some of those things very well right now. That's okay. The more you practice using these tools and skills, the more you will develop resilience. You will get better at them over time, which will help you manage your difficult circumstances more effectively. And as you develop resilience, you will automatically develop more perseverance, too. The two things work together.

Even my short career as a place kicker would not have been possible without resilience. I had to recognize that my skill as a kicker (or lack of) was not a mark of my own value and worth. I had to set smaller goals and work hard to reach them. I had to ask for help and be willing to be coached and taught. And because I did all of those things, I kept going, even when I missed every extra point I attempted. I kept working and driving forward so that, when I did finally make that kick, I was even more prepared to move to the next, harder stage of my comeback.

Perseverance allows you to pursue a powerful and productive new life that is full of passion and opportunity. With a positive mindset, a willingness to try creative solutions, and the perseverance to keep going no matter what, you can meet and rise above any problems you face.

You can Find A Way.

MAKING IT PERSONAL

1. Why can it sometimes be hard to keep moving forward in life? What holds us back?

2. Describe a time when you displayed perseverance. Did having a goal help? What might have happened if you didn't persevere?

3. Do you think laughter can really help us persevere? When has humor helped you through a difficult situation?

4. Resilience is one of the main factors that indicates whether or not someone will succeed. Do you think you show resilience well? Why or why not?

CHAPTER SIX

The Day
I Realized I Was
Living Again

 So that's my story. I lost my hands in an accident, but I discovered that it's always possible to Find A Way. You have to change your mindset. You have to adapt. You have to persevere . . . no matter what. But when you do, you will Find A Way.

Before you put this book down and we go our separate ways, though, I need to say two final things. They're quick, but they are important. Here they are. . . .

Small and Mighty

When I visit a school, I often ask students to meet my original challenge: get a drink from a water bottle without using their hands. I've seen them use their mouths, their elbows, and their knees to get it done. It takes time and sometimes a lot of creativity for them to figure out what to do, especially for the student who popped the top off of his bottle and all the water spilled out (he licked the water off the gym floor!). But I have yet to have a student NOT figure out how to get a drink.

Clearly, this kind of minute-to-win-it challenge isn't a big deal, really. It's an icebreaker. It gets the entire room on the same page. And, let's be honest, it's kind of funny to watch the students who are down on their knees trying to get the task done.

But here's the point: Little things can teach us important lessons. My water bottle was just a small thing. It wasn't terribly remarkable, but it certainly had a huge impact in my life. And most of the challenges that we face when we Find A Way are not earth-shattering. They are very small. They are mundane. They are daily choices and everyday challenges that don't seem very big at the time. They don't seem like they will have much impact at all.

But they do. In reality, those small-but-mighty moments all work together to help us become the people who Find A Way.

They build momentum.

Momentum is a current that carries us forward. You've seen it. It's a big game, and one team is losing badly. Nothing seems to work for them, and the score tells the hard truth. But then, they make a big play. And something changes. There's a shift in energy. The losing team suddenly gains a little confidence while the winning team stumbles. The winning team pushes back, but the losing team makes another play. And another. And suddenly, the entire story is different. The team that had, only moments before, been assured a victory is now faltering. The momentum has changed, and it's suddenly a whole new ballgame.

But it all started because of one play. One play can change the outcome of the game. One moment can change the outcome of your life.

> One moment can change the outcome of your life.

Those small moments create confidence. Each one is only one step, but it is a step. And with each step forward, you get that much closer to your goal. You move farther each time. You move faster. And momentum slowly builds.

Think of a train starting along the tracks. At first it seems like nothing is happening. But then the wheels start to turn. Slowly, the momentum builds until the train cannot be stopped. It works the same way for you. With each step, you gain more confidence. And confidence means you keep pushing. And the pushing creates more momentum until, like that train, you cannot be stopped.

Just look at me. In those first awful minutes and hours, filled with hospitals and helicopters and people speeding through the night to help me, nothing made sense. I thought my life had ended; I was sure my sports career was over. In that dark place, I could not see how I would ever find a way forward to anything meaningful or significant.

But I did. I've come so very far. I played football again and earned all-state honors. I learned to live again, and I learned that there's a lot more to me than I realized before the accident. But most importantly, what I've learned is that Find A Way doesn't require a magic wand. It doesn't require a lot of money. It only requires accepting the one small challenge that each new "water bottle moment" brings.

Those moments are often very small, but their impact is immeasurable. And no matter where you're starting from, and no matter where you hope to end up, when you build momentum, when you take each step forward as it comes, when you combine a transformed mindset with a willingness to adapt and the perseverance to keep going no matter how tough it gets, you will Find A Way. That's all it takes.

Well, almost all.

You Gotta Want It

There are some people who never Find A Way. I met a girl several years ago who lost her leg in a motorcycle accident. She has a prosthetic leg, but she never accepted it. She lives with her mom and stays in a wheelchair. She relies on everyone else around her and never pushed to become independent. And unfortunately, today, she is still stuck right where she was when we first met years ago.

Her problem isn't that she can't Find A Way or that the strategy is somehow flawed. She, and many others like her, has simply missed out on one very important ingredient.

What is it? Coach Shininger said it best: "If you're thirsty enough, you'll find a way."

That's the real issue. You have to want it. You have to want it more than staying where you are. You have to want it badly enough that you go after it, that you fight for it. You have to want it so much that you'll quit coming up with excuses and make the necessary sacrifices that will get you to your goal.

You have to want it.

You have to be thirsty enough ...

> To swallow your pride and ask for help.
> To walk away from the drug scene or party scene that's keeping you distracted.
> To refuse to listen to those people who put you down or that voice in your own head that says, "You aren't good enough."

If you're thirsty enough, you will push yourself harder than you ever thought you could. And I will tell you, you will end up going farther than you ever thought possible.

If you had told me shortly after the accident, after losing my hands, that I would play football again, lead the team in tackles, and earn first-team all-state honors my senior year, I would have thought you were mocking me or just feeding me some wishful thinking. But I did all of those things. I learned, just like Coach Shininger said, that if I wanted it badly enough and was willing to work hard to get it, I could accomplish whatever I put my mind to.

And I'm saying the same thing to you. If you're willing to change your mindset, if you're willing to adapt, if you're willing to persevere . . .

If you're thirsty enough . . .

You will Find A Way.

MAKING IT PERSONAL

1. How can small, mundane decisions or choices help us overcome great obstacles?

2. Make a list of some examples of small choices that might help you keep moving forward. How many of these do you do personally?

3. Coach Shininger said, "If you're thirsty enough, you'll find a way." What does it mean to be "thirsty enough"?

4. We all have areas of life where we need to Find A Way. What needs to change in your life so that you can begin to move forward, even today?

Notes

Chapter 3

[1]See Joel Penton, *Stand Your Ground* (Madison Press, 2010).

[2]Patty O'Grady, "Achievement Vs. Accomplishment," *Psychology Today*, November 11, 2012, https://www.psychologytoday.com/blog/positive-psychology-in-the-classroom/201211/achievement-vs-accomplishment.

[3]My label is actually a legal distinction, too. The state of Ohio has labeled me permanently and totally disabled.

Chapter 4

[1]Webster's Third New International Dictionary, Unabridged, s.v. "adapt," accessed June 30, 2017, http://unabridged.merriam-webster.com.

[2]Jeffrey Baumgartner, "The Basics of Creative Problem Solving," *Innovation Management*, 2017, http://www.innovationmanagement.se/imtool-articles/the-basics-of-creative-problem- solving-cps.

Chapter 5

[1]Pat Forde, "The Complicated Relationships that Molded Michael Phelps into the Greatest," *Yahoo Sports*, Aug. 12, 2016, http://sports.yahoo.com/news/michael-phelps-bob-bowman-greatest-000000911.html.

[2]Megan Bruneau, "These 7 Qualities Lead to Perseverance When Faced with Adversity," *Forbes.com,* September 26, 2016, https://www.forbes.com/sites/meganbruneau/2016/09/25/ these-7-qualities-lead-to-perseverance-when-faced-with-adversity/#49bd48712f82.

[3]Cynthia Thaik, "Laughter Improves Overall Health," *Psychology Today,* January 20, 2014, https://www.psychologytoday.com/blog/the-heart/201401/laughter-improves-overall-health-0.

[4]Thaik, "Laughter Improves Overall Health."

[5]"The Road to Resilience," *American Psychological Association,* 2017, http://www.apa.org/ helpcenter/road-resilience.aspx.

[6]Brad Waters, "10 Traits of Emotionally Resilient People," *Psychology Today,* May 21, 2013, https://www.psychologytoday.com/blog/design-your-path/201305/10-traits-emotionally-resilient-people.